The Beach Bum's Guide to the

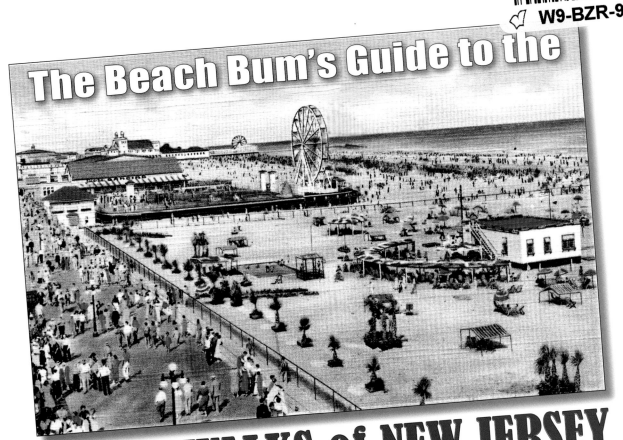

BOARDWALKS of NEW JERSEY

Dick Handschuch and Sal Marino

DOWN THE SHORE
PUBLISHING
WEST CREEK, NJ

Box 100, West Creek, NJ 08092
www.down-the-shore.com
Down The Shore Books LLC / Down The Shore Publishing
The words "Down The Shore" and the Down The Shore Publishing
logos are registered U.S. Trademarks.

Book and cover design by Leslee Ganss
Caricatures by Glenn Juszczak
Printed in China
10 9 8 7 6 5 4 3
Revised 3rd edition, 2023

Library of Congress Cataloging-in-Publication Data
Handschuch, Dick.
Beach bum's guide to the boardwalks of New Jersey / Dick Handschuch and Sal Marino.
    p. cm.
Includes bibliographical references.
ISBN 1-59322-037-5
    1. Recreation--New Jersey--Guidebooks. 2. Boardwalks--New Jersey--Guidebooks. 3. New Jersey--Description and travel. I. Marino, Sal (Sal A). II. Title.
GV53.H27 2007
917.4904--dc22
                    2008007687

ISBN-13 978-1-59322-037-2

To our wives, Carol and Barbara,
for their encouragement
and help.

Contents

"This all goes into that potpourri that helps future generations understand what this was all about — what it is all about. It should always be preserved and this book will help...."

— Atlantic City historian and archivist Vicki Gold Levi in *The Press of Atlantic City*

The Atlantic City Boardwalk at the Steel Pier in the 1930s.

Preface

When we first planned to walk all the boardwalks of New Jersey (Why? Because they were there!), we visited our county library and found there was no complete list available. So we decided to develop our own list and include not only location but length, composition, accessibility and other features to serve as a reference for other walkers. And so this book was born.

As we trod the boardwalks we discovered they come in all sizes and styles. We started to ask questions about history, how the walks were constructed and what happened to the ones we remembered from our youth. Most of our questions were answered, and we hope yours will be, too.

We wanted the book to be more than just a list. In the end it took us longer to complete the book than it did to walk all the boardwalks. We had to deal with changes that were occurring as we wrote. Besides repairing the boards or replacing brick pavers, municipalities were changing the contours of the seaside by replenishing the sand.

While many beaches received new sand these past years, none has changed the landscape as much as the Long Branch beachfront. When we first came upon this boardwalk we reported how high the walk was from the ocean. "Here as you walk on a high bluff you look down upon the sea," we wrote. Today the boardwalk sits just above the sand and there is a fine, wide sandy beach that stretches to the water. Since then we've revisited several sites and have updated this new edition to reflect any changes we encountered.

We also met many fascinating people who shared their stories with us. You, too, will meet fellow travelers as you use this guide, perhaps even us. So if you see two guys (one short, plenty of hair; the other tall, no hair) just wave "hello" as you walk the "boards" of the Jersey Shore.

— *Dick Handschuch and Sal Marino*

Arriving on the boardwalk in Ocean City.

Atlantic City's Convention Hall (today called Boardwalk Hall), the Boardwalk, hotels, and piers in 1937. A note on back of this postcard says, "Loads of fun! Dad and I are here and he's enjoying it heaps too!"

A Short History of the Boardwalks of the Jersey Shore

During the early 1800s, the few towns found at the Jersey Shore remained unchanged — small fishing hamlets with perhaps a few hunting lodges in the marshes. By the late 1800s, though, as railroads made shore towns more accessible to visitors from New York and Philadelphia, more and more people began to come.

Railroad connections were developed in the 1850s, largely through the efforts of Dr. Jonathan Pitney of Absecon, who was convinced that the people of Philadelphia could benefit from the healthy qualities of the sea at Absecon Beach. Pitney and his association set about building Atlantic City and part of the Camden and Atlantic Railroad went into operation on July 1, 1854.

Several railroads were con-

Mr. Peanut

For nearly 79 years, Mr. Peanut greeted people on the Atlantic City Boardwalk. Like Mickey Mouse welcoming all to Disneyworld, Mr. Peanut was the official greeter in front of the Planter's Peanuts store. People would always stop to shake his hand or to have their picture taken with him.

The high-hat character with his monocle can still be seen today, preserved behind glass at the Atlantic City Museum in Boardwalk Hall.

structed along the north Jersey coast, and by the end of the 1880s, Long Beach Island, Seaside Park, Brigantine, Ocean City, Ludlam's Beach and Five Mile Beach (now Wildwood) were connected to the mainland by rails.

Hotel owners and railroad conductors became concerned about all the beach sand that was being tracked onto lobby carpets and into railroad cars. Planks of wood were temporarily laid on the sand as a walkway and were removed at the end of the season.

The Civil War interrupted development and postponed, for a while, the tourist boom. War-damaged railroads needed the iron rails, so local interests had to wait.

Although Atlantic City

usually gets the credit, it was in Cape May that the first boards were laid down, in 1868. Atlantic City followed in 1870 and, later, was the first to raise its boardwalk.

As more and more people flocked to the shore, the need for a more permanent type of structure became apparent. Planners had to cope with the surf, the tides and access to the streets. "Build it and they will come" seemed to be their motto. The longer the boardwalk, the better.

In his 1889 book, *The New Jersey Coast and Pines,* writer Gustav Kobbe talks of the boards at Asbury Park and Ocean Grove: "Along the beach there is a well-kept plank walk one mile long, with seats and pavilions at intervals, joining the esplanade of Ocean Grove, thus giving an unbroken promenade of nearly two miles."

As the seats and pavilions filled with people, eateries began to spring up. Tourists could walk the boardwalks, enjoy the views and, when the time came, find a snack or even dinner close by.

Boardwalks quickly became permanent structures

Riding along the boards in Ocean City.

Asbury Park Convention Center and 7th Avenue pavilion in a 1937 postcard view.

in many shore towns. This meant that they had to be maintained throughout the year, whether they were used only in the summer or during cold winters as well.

The first boardwalk built on pilings in Ocean County was at Point Pleasant Beach in the 1890s. Permanent boardwalks were also constructed at Seaside Park, Bay Head, Lavallette and Beach Haven.

By the early 1900s many shore towns had planked walks, boardwalks or promenades. What had once been a practical means of getting to and from the beaches became a place to stroll, watch people, and congregate. Here you could show off your finery, mingle with the rich and famous, meet your sweetie, enjoy the sun without getting sand in your shoes, chew salt water taffy and ogle the growing number of sights along the boards.

As the crowds grew, so did the businesses. Today boardwalks are where visitors go to enjoy rides, amusements, games of chance, arcades, and, of course, to shop and eat.

The first boardwalk amusements were built in the 1870s in Atlantic City. They were soon followed by fishing and amusement piers. Point Pleasant Beach and Seaside Heights began offering dozens of entertainments. Few resorts could resist the lure of the boards, though some, such as Long Beach Island, kept commercialism to a minimum.

Atlantic City, whose boardwalk is the only one written with a capital "B", quickly became the entertainment mecca of the Jersey Shore and adopted the motto "America's Playground." Sylvester B. Butler, a teacher from Pleasantville, wrote his mother in August of 1916:

"The Boardwalk is a very wide, substantial affair, about nine miles long, being from fifty to a hundred feet from the water's edge all along. On the side away from the beach are the hotels and then all kinds of shops,

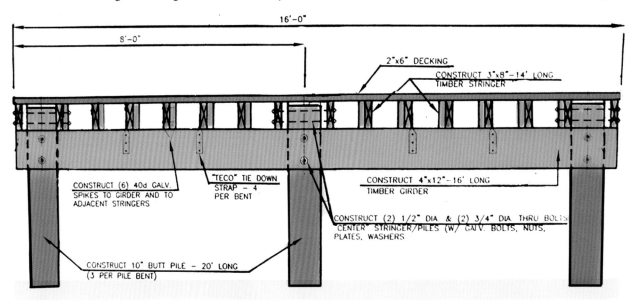

Cross section of a modern wooden boardwalk.

such as one would find in any city, except that I would say there were more soda fountains and candy shops than on a regular city street; then there are some moving picture theaters, merry- go-rounds, shooting galleries, and other amusement places; also any number of what I suppose might be called terminals for the wheeled chairs...bath houses are also on that side of the walk; and to get from them to the beach you go under the walk — I don't believe you ever see anybody on the walk with their bathing suit. On the beach side of the walk, there are here and there long piers reaching out into the ocean, and on these piers are the principal amusement places of Atlantic City."

And, from a publicity brochure: "Atlantic City's Boardwalk is a metropolis in itself, a metropolis of joy, a metropolis of amusement, a metropolis of health, a metropolis of wonderful sights that can be seen in no other place in the world except on the Boardwalk in Atlantic City."

Boardwalks evolved from a practical way of getting to and from the beach to a commercial enterprise carrying tourists from hotels to hawkers.

"At the entrance [to Steel Pier] you are charged 10 cents thru the day, 15 cents at night, and this entitles you to the run of the pier; there are countless numbers of people going in all the time, and as they continue to run, I imagine there's no money lost in the scheme, but you certainly get a good deal for your money," according to Butler.

Today, boardwalks are used all year long as a more active public jogs or just walks for pleasure and health, and New Jersey offers a variety of boardwalks to meet the needs of everyone.

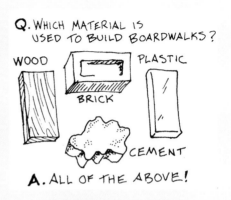

The Trouble With Wood

Walking the Jersey "boards" you will notice a variety of materials used by each town. Brick, macadam, interlocking pavers, cement, plastic and, of course, wood are common materials. Though wood has been traditional since boards were first laid on the sand, it isn't always the best choice.

The problem with wood is that it wears, weathers and splinters. If not replaced, the planks become narrower and more difficult to walk on. Recycled plastic and other materials last longer. Yet, when we reminisce about boardwalks, wood is what we remember. It retains the history of the boardwalks and, as many towns continue to use wood, it carries the tradition into the future as well.

Asbury Park in its heyday, circa 1900, in a colorful postcard view.

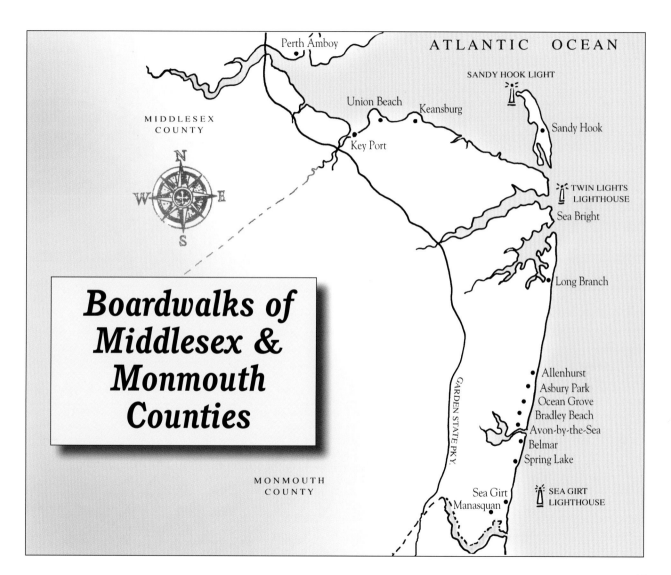

ATLANTIC OCEAN

Perth Amboy

SANDY HOOK LIGHT

Union Beach   Keansburg

MIDDLESEX
COUNTY

Sandy Hook

N

Key Port

W   E

S

TWIN LIGHTS
LIGHTHOUSE

Sea Bright

Long Branch

**Boardwalks of
Middlesex &
Monmouth
Counties**

GARDEN STATE PKY.

Allenhurst
Asbury Park
Ocean Grove
Bradley Beach
Avon-by-the-Sea
Belmar
Spring Lake

MONMOUTH
COUNTY

Sea Girt
Manasquan

SEA GIRT
LIGHTHOUSE

15

Traditional Boardwalks & Promenades

Sea Bright

Length: 0.25 miles

The town has a very large rock and concrete sea wall running along the ocean. One cannot see the beach or have an ocean view due to the wall's height. Parking in the center of the town's municipal lot gives you access to the sea wall's promenade. Walking on top of the sea wall you get a complete view of the beach, the ocean, ships, and distant Long Island. Once you come to the end of the promenade, do not continue. The sea wall is wide, but does not have any rails along the sides, plus the unevenness of the rock and cement make it unsafe to walk.

Directions:

Take Garden State Parkway exit 117 to Route 36 to the ocean. As you cross over from Highlands keep to the left for Sea Bright or to the right for Sandy Hook Gateway National Park.

Long Branch

Length: 2.2 miles

South of Seven Presidents Oceanfront Park is the beginning of the "promenade." This walkway is approximately twenty feet wide, made of large, square brick pavers — each about two feet — running over a half-mile before it becomes composite board. This walk is one of the highest in New Jersey, sitting atop a

The Seven President Residents

Along the promenade you can stop to admire the monuments to the seven U.S. presidents that summered in Long Branch. The center monument is a life-size, standing statue of James Garfield, our twentieth president, who died here in 1881.

Others are for Ulysses S. Grant, eighteenth president, from 1869 to 1877, who vacationed for twelve years at 991 Ocean Avenue, which was known as "The Summer Capitol"; Rutherford B. Hayes, nineteenth president, from 1877 to 1881; Chester Arthur, twenty-first president, from 1881 to 1885; Benjamin Harrison, twenty-third president, from 1889 to 1893; William McKinley, twenty-fifth president, from 1897 to 1901; and Woodrow Wilson, twenty-eighth president, from 1913 to 1921.

Long Branch was the high-fashion spot on the Jersey Shore in 1905.

high sand bluff. However, after beach replenishment projects brought sand up to the boardwalk, it does not have that "looking-down-on-the-water" feeling anymore except at the south end.

Directions:

Take Garden State Parkway exit 105 to Route 36 east, which becomes Joline Avenue, to Ocean Avenue. Seven Presidents Oceanfront Park in North Long Branch is straight ahead. Turn south for the Long Branch boardwalk, which is just east of Ocean Avenue.

The Asbury Park boardwalk today, looking north from inside the historic Casino building, built in 1929.

Allenhurst
Length: 0.2 miles

This small boardwalk sits high above the ocean where one can peer down upon the surf. Looking south you can see Asbury Park, while to the north rise the Deal jetties. Many benches line the walk for a relaxed view of the Atlantic Ocean.

Directions:

Coming from the north, take Garden State Parkway exit 102. Go east on Asbury Avenue and follow to its end at Ocean Avenue. Take Ocean Avenue north until you go around Deal Lake and follow Ocean Avenue again. Stay on Ocean Avenue until you reach Corlies Avenue, then make a right to the boardwalk.

From the south, take exit 100A to Route 66 east, follow until you reach Asbury Avenue. Follow directions above for Long Branch.

Asbury Park
Length: 0.9 miles

The Asbury Park boardwalk has been replaced with new wood and the entire oceanfront area is in the process of being revitalized. Walking the

The Morro Castle, beached by the Asbury Park boardwalk in September 1934.

The S.S. Morro Castle
Disaster

It's not often that a New Jersey boardwalk outside of Atlantic City receives widespread attention. However Asbury Park's boardwalk gave an international audience a front row seat when the luxury ocean liner *Morro Castle,* sailing from Havana to New York, consumed in a raging fire, drifted onto the city's beach on September 8, 1934.

The town capitalized on the tragedy that killed 137 as the smoldering, stranded ship became a tourist attraction. Over a million came to see it; hawkers sold souvenirs and photographs, and the dramatic story filled front pages for weeks.

The Casino in Asbury Park was designed for dancing, not gambling.

"boards," one cannot help but notice the improvements along the newly-bustling boardwalk.

The original promenade, built in 1880, was 2000 feet long with a band pavilion. There were plans to put in an aquarium on the ocean side, too, but the city decided it would block the view. They argued for ten years over the building of Convention Hall, which was finally finished in 1930, just in time for the Depression.

The present walk will take you through Convention Hall and past candy shops and end at the empty grand Casino structure that once housed an elaborate carousel.

Directions:

Use the directions for Allenhurst (previous page) to Ocean Avenue. Boardwalk is east of Ocean Avenue.

On the oceanfront in Asbury Park it was horse vs. horseless carriages.

Ocean Grove
Length: 0.7 miles

To head south on the Ocean Grove boardwalk, start at the south side of the Asbury Park Casino. Reconstructed after Superstorm Sandy, the town has a new boardwalk made of composite boards. There are many benches along the way made of recycled plastic on cement legs. The Camp Meeting Association has maintained the town's historic look for years.

This can be seen in the charming wood-framed homes and hotels — a big contrast to the modern appearance of Asbury Park to the north.

Directions:
Garden State Parkway from the south, take exit 100B. Coming from the north, take exit 100. Follow Route 33 east to Main Street. Enter Ocean Grove on Main Street, follow to Ocean Avenue; the boardwalk is east of Ocean Avenue.

The boardwalk at Avon-by-the-Sea has plenty of resting spots.

Bradley Beach

Length: 0.8 miles

Beginning in Ocean Grove and walking south through Bradley Beach, you stroll along a clean, high, bulkheaded boardwalk composed of brick pavers. Work is being done to improve the oceanfront in Bradley Beach. You will pass a miniature golf course right on the boardwalk as well as a bandstand with plenty of benches to accommodate summer crowds. Throughout the course of the walk there are many wooden and cement benches.

Directions:

Follow the directions for Ocean Grove (previous page) but at Main Street go south. Turn left on Newark Avenue and head east to Ocean Avenue.

Avon-by-the-Sea
Length: 0.5 miles

A half-mile of well-kept boardwalk straddles the beach while the bulkhead on the west side borders the road. You can walk south right up to the Shark River Inlet and view the waterway from a small pavilion. Immediately to the south of the inlet is Belmar. However, looking further south one can see as far as Point Pleasant Beach and the Manasquan Inlet, catching a glimpse of the condominiums that sit at the north end of the Point Pleasant Beach boardwalk.

Twin Lights of the Navesink

Just off Route 36, take Highlands Avenue to Lighthouse Road to the Twin Lights State Historic Site, the first electrically operated lighthouse in the United States. Built in 1862, it is on one of the highest points on the eastern seaboard and offers a spectacular view of New York City and the surrounding bay area. There is also a maritime history museum.

Side Trips
Fort Hancock
(Gateway, Sandy Hook)

At Gateway National Recreation Area there's a Coast Guard Museum that explores the history of the U.S. Lifesaving Service, the Coast Guard's predecessor.

From there, visit the country's oldest operating lighthouse, Sandy Hook Lighthouse in Fort Hancock. Walk to the various gun batteries, which offer excellent views from the observation deck, and explore the many buildings in and around the fort.

Royal Governor's Mansion

This National Historic Registry building, also known as Proprietary House, was built around 1764. New Jersey's last Royal Governor, William Franklin, lived here before the Revolutionary War. It is the only remaining official governor's residence from the days of the original thirteen colonies. Located at 149 Kearny Avenue in Perth Amboy.

Royal Governor's Mansion

Belmar's boardwalk.

Directions:

Use the directions for Ocean Grove (page 21). At Main Street go south to Lakeside Avenue. Make a left and proceed to Ocean Avenue.

Belmar
Length: 1.3 miles

This boardwalk is composed mostly of recycled plastic with composite boards. Walking along the beachfront you pass a mix of homes and businesses, just west of the road. To the east of the mile-plus walk there are several playgrounds at the edge of the beach. Work has been done on the northern end to widen the boardwalk.

Directions:

Take Garden State Parkway exit 98 to Route 138 east, then follow Route 35 north to 11th Avenue in Belmar. Make a right (east) and follow to Ocean Avenue.

In 1933 you could watch U.S. Navy and other blimps pass by over the fishing pier in Belmar.

The boardwalk at Spring Lake.

Spring Lake
Length: 1.8 miles

If you begin your walk at the northern end you may meet many other walkers and a few joggers. The boardwalk is made of composite boards and has protective sand dunes along the western side of the walk so one can see the beach and ocean. There are benches facing the ocean about every twenty-five feet, and the boardwalk is bordered by an iron railing on both sides.

Along the walk there are two swimming pools with changing rooms, as well as the Spring Lake Bath and Tennis Club on the west side of Ocean Avenue. An underground passageway

Side Trips
Monmouth Beach Cultural Center

This old Coast Guard Station showcases local art and shore history. It is located on Ocean Avenue (Route 36) in Monmouth Beach.

Sea Girt Lighthouse

This lighthouse at Ocean Avenue and Beacon Boulevard was built in 1896 and restored in 1991, and houses historic displays and lighthouse artifacts. It was the nation's first lighthouse to be equipped with a radio fog signal.

Monmouth University (Wilson Hall)

Just west of the Long Branch boardwalk lies the Monmouth University campus. This wonderfully landscaped estate offers the Erlenger Garden which has a water organ modeled on "la Colonade" at Versailles.

Woodrow Wilson Hall has been designated a National Historic Landmark. In 1981, the building was the scene for the filming of *Annie*, serving as the Park Avenue mansion of the character Daddy Warbucks.

A self-guided tour is available during the day by following an excellent guide prepared by the Office of University Communications, which may be picked up in the lobby of Wilson Hall. Guggenheim Memorial Library is located at the university. The library is also modeled after Versailles and is listed in the National Register of Historic Places

Ocean Grove National Historic District Pathway to the Great Auditorium

The town of Ocean Grove has many Victorian buildings which can be seen by touring the area. The Historical Society of Ocean Grove, located at 50 Pitman Avenue, can assist with specific tours. Visit the Ocean Grove Camp Meeting Association, 54 Pitman Avenue, for information and available tours of the Great Auditorium.

Allaire State Park

Although this state park is a few miles west of the boardwalks, it is an excellent side trip. Located on Route 524 in Wall Township, it recreates a 19th-century ironworking village. Homes, a bakery, a blacksmith shop and a general store all provide a look into the past.

The Visitor's Center, picnic area, and nature center round out the offerings.

takes you under Ocean Avenue to the beach. The old Essex and Sussex Hotel has been converted into condominiums and next door where the Monmouth Hotel once stood there are private residences. The homes along Ocean Avenue are some of the most beautiful on the Jersey Shore.

Directions:

Same as Belmar (page 24), but at Route 35 head south to Allaire Road. Turn left (east) and cross Route 71 where Allaire Road becomes Ludlow Avenue. Follow Ocean Avenue south to Spring Lake.

Sea Girt
Length: 0.7 miles

You can begin just across the street from the old Sea Girt Lighthouse (see Side Trips), built in 1886 and restored in 1981. The boardwalk has the most benches of any in Monmouth County and there are many beautiful homes along the way. The southern end of the boardwalk passes Cornelius Park.

Directions:

Same as Belmar (page 24). At Route 71 turn right (south) to Beacon Boulevard, make a left (east) and take to Ocean Avenue.

Manasquan
Length: 0.8 miles

The macadam promenade along the oceanfront is just short of one mile long. The beach is exceptionally wide here thanks to a massive restoration effort and

Strictly speaking, it's not a boardwalk in Perth Amboy, but these people don't seem to mind in this old postcard view.

features small dunes along the east side of the walk. If you are lucky you might see the pounding surf careening off the north jetty rocks of Manasquan Inlet, which is the entrance to the Intracoastal Waterway.

Directions:

Garden State Parkway to exit 98, then Route 34 south to Route 524 east. This becomes Atlantic Avenue. Follow Atlantic Avenue to Broad Street and turn right (south) to Main Street. Make a left (east) on Main Street and follow it to Ocean Avenue.

Under the Boardwalk$

The authors remember a time when kids needed money and would crawl under the boardwalk to search for change. Coins, especially quarters, that fell through the cracks would land standing vertical in the sand and could easily be spotted and collected. Sifting through the sand could locate enough money for a fun evening on the boardwalk.

Other Walks

Perth Amboy
Length: 1.0 miles

This mile long "boardwalk" is made of attractive red brick pavers. It is about seven feet wide and wraps around the Kill Van Kull in a southerly direction, then runs west along Raritan Bay. It offers a beautiful view of Staten Island, the New Jersey Highlands and the South Amboy waterfront. The western end of the walkway ends near the north shore railroad bridge.

Directions:
From the north or south, take the Garden State Parkway to exit 127 or Route 9 and follow signs to Perth Amboy. Follow signs for Smith Street which will take you to the waterfront.

Keyport
Length: 0.5 miles

The walk along the waterfront is macadam over a newly bulit sea wall. Along the way you can rest on concrete benches to enjoy excellent views of Staten Island, the Verrazano Narrows Bridge and the Brooklyn and Manhattan skyline.

Directions:
Take Garden State Parkway exit 117 then go south on Route 36, following signs for Keyport. Turn either on Main Street or Broad Street and follow it to the waterfront.

Union Beach
Length: 0.35 miles

Union Beach is "where the crime rate is the lowest in New Jersey," according to one resident. It also offers a 3000-foot macadam walkway perched above a high bulkhead overlooking a sandy beach, and affords a great view of Raritan Bay.

Directions:
Take Garden State Parkway exit 117, then go south on Route 36 to Union Avenue. Take Union Avenue to the beachfront at Front Street where the walkway begins.

Keansburg
(no boardwalk)

The amusements are still there in Keansburg and the fishing pier remains but there is no longer any boardwalk. There is a macadam walkway through the amusement area which is closed during the winter. A wooden bay walk over the dunes lies east and west of the amusements.

Directions:
Take Garden State Parkway exit 117 and head south on Route 36 to Laurel Avenue. Take Laurel north to Beachway. The amusements are on the left side.

Ocean Parks

Sandy Hook
Length: 100 yards

In this section of the Gateway National Recreation Area, managed by the National Park Service, there is a wooden walk which is west of the main road and opposite the old rescue station. Set high over the marsh, it affords an excellent view of Spermaceti Cove and the Highlands.

Seven Presidents County Park
Length: 0.2 miles

Driving into North Long Branch at its north end you come upon Seven Presidents County Park which has a short wooden walkway along the beachfront that cuts through a natural habitat of plants.

Directions:

Take Garden State Parkway exit 105 to Route 36 east, which becomes Joline Avenue, to Ocean Avenue. Head north on Ocean — the park entrance is on the right.

Heel Savers

During the late 1940s and through the early '60s women would walk the boardwalk dressed in their finest, no matter what the temperature. Of course, high heels were worn, which was a problem when these thin heels got caught in the spaces between the boards.

To alleviate this, five-and-dime stores sold rubber tips to be placed over the heel of the shoe, which made the heel wider than the opening between the planks, so women could avoid getting stuck in the "boards".

The Curtain

During the Second World War, New Jersey boardwalks had a fifteen-foot-high blackout curtain, which ran along the east side of the boards dividing the boardwalk from the beach and the ocean.

These curtains were drawn up by day, allowing visitors to see the water. At night the curtains were lowered so the enemy could not directly see the lights from all of the amusements.

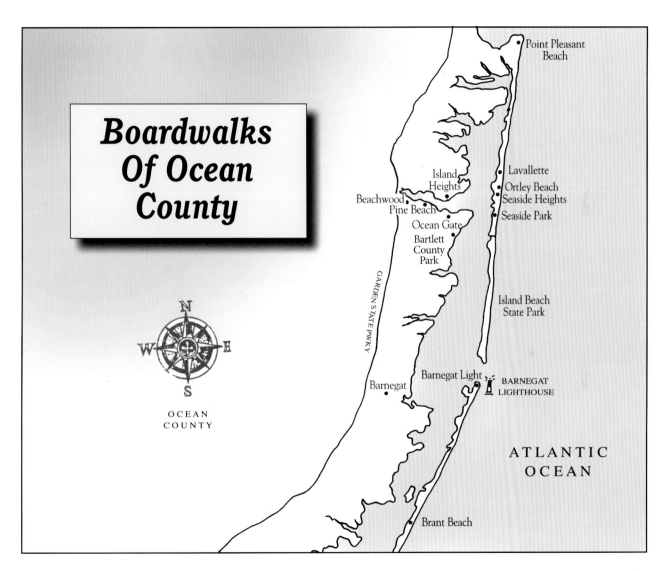

Boardwalks Of Ocean County

Point Pleasant Beach

Island Heights

Lavallette
Ortley Beach
Seaside Heights

Beachwood
Pine Beach
Seaside Park

Ocean Gate

Bartlett County Park

Island Beach State Park

GARDEN STATE PWKY

N
W E
S

OCEAN COUNTY

Barnegat Light
BARNEGAT LIGHTHOUSE

Barnegat

ATLANTIC OCEAN

Brant Beach

Traditional Boardwalks & Promenades

The boardwalk at Point Pleasant Beach offers a moveable feast.

Point Pleasant Beach

Length: 1.0 miles

Walking here at any time of the year you can encounter strollers and spot surfers in the ocean. The boardwalk widens from its normal fifteen feet to about thirty-five feet at the amusement area. Begin your walk at the north end of the boardwalk, which is on the south side of the Manasquan Inlet, where you can watch boats maneuver toward the Intracoastal Waterway. The walk continues to its southern end at New Jersey Avenue.

Directions:

Coming from the north, take exit 98 on the Garden State Parkway to Route 34 south. At Route 35 continue south to Broadway then east to Ocean Avenue. Coming from the south, take exit 90 on the Garden State Parkway. This brings you to Chambers Bridge Road. Follow this to Route 70, make a left and go east to Route 88 east. When you cross over the Veterans Memorial Bridge make a left on Arnold Avenue and follow this through town to Ocean Avenue.

Lavalette

Length: 1.3 miles

The boardwalk begins at Ortley Avenue on the north end and continues to Dover Avenue on the southern side of town. It is about 15 feet wide with benches facing the east. Homes crowd close to the boardwalk on the west. The eastern side is bordered by high sand dunes planted with cord grass.

Directions:

Take Garden State Parkway exit 82 for Route 37 east. Cross the Bay Bridge and take Route 35 north to Lavallette and take any street east to boardwalk.

A Moveable Walk

The first boardwalk in Point Pleasant Beach, in 1880, was "portable" — planks laid in the sand and taken up at the end of the season. While other resorts soon built more permanent structures (Atlantic City was the first), it wasn't until 1912 that this town decided to fasten the middle 400 feet of their walk on pilings. It took another decade or so to secure the rest of it.

The beach in Seaside Heights looks pretty much the same today, but the boardwalk is bigger.

Ortley Beach
Length: 0.4 miles

The boardwalk is in two sections, separated in the middle by private property with some new homes. Each section is approximately two-tenths of a mile long, bordered on both sides by four-foot rails and benches along the way. The north end begins at First Avenue and ends at Coolidge Avenue. One must walk in the street from 5th Avenue to 7th Avenue before getting to the other section.

Directions:

Same as Lavallette. At Coolidge Avenue go east to Ocean Terrace.

Seaside Heights

Length: 0.8 miles

The combined boardwalks of Seaside Heights and Seaside Park give you two-and-one-half-miles of continuous shore views. As you start at the north end of the Heights you will notice amusements and game stands on the western side, and low sand dunes on the eastern side. There are only two areas where the ocean cannot be seen — the Casino Pier at the north and The Beach Club at the south end. Off-season strollers will be happy to learn there are restrooms open all year.

Directions:

Garden State Parkway exit 82 to Route 37 east. When you cross over Bay Bridge follow signs to Seaside Heights beach.

Seaside Park

Length: 1.7 miles

The northern end of this boardwalk continues with the amusements, which spill over from the Heights. But once they end, there is a mile and a half of open boardwalk with dunes on the east side. The walk is pleasant, and as the high dunes obstruct the

Seaside Park is where the quiet is.

Side Trips

Point Pleasant Beach Inland Waterway and Inlet

At the north end of the boardwalk the Inland Waterway begins. Here at the Manasquan Inlet you can see boats entering the ocean or returning from fishing.

In the northeast end of this town you can also find seafood restaurants and admire the small seaport that berths commercial ocean fishing boats.

Jenkinson's Aquarium

On the Point Pleasant Beach boardwalk you will find this small but excellent aquarium. In addition to local marine life, it has an array of coral reef fish, harbor seals, exotic birds and amphibians, and sharks. There is also a hands-on section for children to enjoy, with a touch-tank, crafts, guided learning center and scheduled seal and penguin feedings.

view of the ocean you can look west at the elegant Ocean Avenue homes.

Directions:

Same as Seaside Heights but when you cross over Bay Bridge follow signs to Seaside Park. You will be on Central Avenue. Take any street east to Ocean Avenue.

Other Walks

Island Heights

Length: 0.5 miles

The Island Heights boardwalk continues along the north bank of the Toms River. Victorian homes sit high along the northern edge of the street that borders the walkway. A casual visitor to New Jersey would not recognize the quaint beauty of this area as part of the Jersey Shore.

Directions:

Take Garden State Parkway exit 82 to Route 37, then go east to Island Heights. Take Central Avenue right (south) to the end.

Beachwood

Length: 0.3 miles

Beachwood has a short, raised boardwalk over the water along the Toms River with high, wooden railings the whole length. It has benches, small docks

The boardwalk in Seaside Park, circa 1902, hasn't changed very much.

and a boat ramp and offers a fine view of the river.

Directions:

Garden State Parkway exit 81 to Water Street east. Take Route 166 south to Beachwood Boulevard and make a left to the end.

Pine Beach

Length: 0.3 miles

This new walk is the beginning of a planned mile-long River Walk along the Toms River, where a good view of the river can be seen.

Directions:

Same as Beachwood but continue on Clubhouse Road to first stop sign, make a left on Motor Road to the river.

Head-Over-Heels

Many boardwalks in the past did not have rails along their edges and in the early 1960s Bay Head had a boardwalk twelve feet above the sand without rails. Sam, a lifeguard at that time, remembers a man walking the boards early one morning. As the man continued his walk, he looked below and saw a girl lying on her stomach sunning herself on her blanket. She had removed the top of her bathing suit to get a full tan on her back. The guards watched as the man was so engrossed with the view that he walked off the boardwalk into thin air and fell to the sand below. The guards ran to assist him, but he said that he was fine, just hurt from embarrassment.

Side Trips

Island Beach State Park

Just south of Seaside there is a ten-mile natural area which offers a vast unspoiled barrier island beach, complete with all the flora and fauna missing from the overdeveloped shore areas.

When entering the park ask for the pamphlet called "Discovery Trails of Island Beach State Park" to help you find the many self-guided trails in the park. A description of the island's plant communities is also available at the Aeolium Nature Center.

Ocean County Historical Society Museum

Approximately eight miles west of the boardwalk, in Toms River, is the county's museum. Housed in a Victorian building are many artifacts of early history and other local exhibits. It is located at 26 Hadley Avenue.

Toms River Seaport Society Museum

This museum is located at Hooper Avenue and Water Street in Toms River. Here one can further their knowledge of the maritime history of Barnegat Bay. Boats, artifacts and memorabilia complete the seaport museum.

As simple as a boardwalk can get, in Ocean Gate.

Ocean Gate
Length: 1.05 miles

Walking along the waterfront of Ocean Gate, which runs along the south bank of the mouth of the Toms River, one sees a new, rebuilt boardwalk — following damage in Superstorm Sandy — as well as an occasional patch of concrete. It is just over a mile long. Erosion has taken its toll in several places, and in some spots the walk is over rocks rather than sand. However, it is a pleasant walk, and you view small bungalows and the beach along the way.

Directions:

Garden State Parkway exit 81. Continue south on Route 9. Take jughandle at Korman Road to cross Route 9. When crossing is made, turn left onto Ocean Gate Drive and follow it to the end. Make a right at Chelsea Avenue for one block, then a left on Ocean Gate Avenue to the boardwalk.

John C. Bartlett Jr. County Park
Length: 0.25 miles

South of the Toms River, John C. Bartlett County Park (formerly Berkeley Island County Park) peninsula juts far out into Barnegat Bay. Its western shore affords an amazing view north, south and especially east, showing the grand expanse of ten-mile long Island Beach State Park.

Directions:

Garden State Parkway exit 77, follow signs to Route 9. Continue south on Route 9 and make a left (east) on Harbor Inn Road and then another left on Neary Avenue. At Brennan Concourse go right and follow it to the end.

Barnegat Municipal Dock
Length: 0.1 miles

Further south, at Barnegat, a small two-story pavilion and a short waterside boardwalk provide good views of the bay and the beautiful expanse of Long Beach Island. The walk follows a newly constructed bulkhead along the western side of Barnegat Bay.

Directions:

From the north, take exit 67 on the Garden State Parkway to Route 554 east passing over Route 9 at the traffic light. Continue straight on East Bay Avenue for a little over a mile and a half. The Municipal Dock is on the right side.

From the south, exit at Garden State Parkway exit 63 and head east on Route 72 until you meet Route 9. Take this north through Manahawkin until you reach Route 554 in Barnegat. Make a right at the traffic light onto East Bay Avenue and follow as above.

Side Trips

Barnegat Light Museum & Edith Duff Gwinn Gardens

In Barnegat Light, the museum on Fifth Street and Central Avenue was a former one-room schoolhouse. This building contains the original 1859 Fresnal lens of the lighthouse, salvaged items from shipwrecks and many historical exhibits. Stroll through the lovely adjacent gardens.

Long Beach Island Historical Association Museum (Beach Haven)

While on Long Beach Island we suggest you make a trip to the south end. The museum building was the first church on the island and houses artifacts and exhibits from Long Beach Island's rich history. Head south on Long Beach Boulevard to Beach Haven; the museum is on Beach and Engleside avenues.

Long Beach Township's Brant Beach observation pavillion, at the end of a short wooden walkway, offers spectacular views.

Brant Beach

Length: 330 feet

This short wooden walk is located on Long Beach Island. Its high platform offers a 110-foot observation deck above the sea and sand. The height also affords a spectacular view of Barnegat Bay which lies to the west of a fine, bayfront park just across the boulevard.

Directions:

Garden State Parkway exit 63 to Route 72 east to Long Beach Island. Turn right on Long Beach Boulevard and head south until 68th Street — you'll see Bayview Park on your right and the Long Beach Township municipal building on your left. The deck is behind the township building on the oceanfront.

Ocean Parks

You can walk the boardwalks at Island Beach State Park from the bayside to the oceanside.

Island Beach State Park

Length: 0.6 miles

Though there is no boardwalk along the beach in this state park, it does have wooden walks across the peninsula from the ocean to the bay. The natural beauty of the dunes, the flora, an occasional red fox and the wild expanse of the ocean and bay make this place unique.

Approximately five miles south of the park's entrance you will find parking area A-7. Here the narrow Fisherman's Walkway runs from the bay to the ocean for two tenths of a mile. It is suggested you take the western section first for a panoramic view of Barnegat Bay and the western shoreline of the pinelands.

The walk over to the ocean takes you through a cross section of the natural barrier beach where illustrated signs explain the wildlife. The walk ends with exquisite views of dunes, sand, and ocean. If you want to see more, park at the North Pavilion (the first parking area you come to, three miles from the entrance) and walk from either side of the building along a wooden walk above the sand to the beach.

Directions:

Garden State Parkway exit 82 to Route 37 east. After crossing the Bay Bridge, stay to the right and follow signs to the park.

Barnegat Lighthouse State Park
Length: 0.5 miles

This walk begins at the parking lot, passes the famous lighthouse and continues out along a cement walkway perched on part of the south jetty of Barnegat Inlet. Here you can watch the many boats passing through and also get a full view of the north jetty on Island Beach State Park, as well as a majestic view of the lighthouse. To the south is a vast expanse of sand formed by the new jetty which provides habitat for many shore birds.

Directions:

Take Garden State Parkway exit 63 to Route 72

Barnegat Lighthouse State Park on Long Beach Island.

east. After crossing the causeway bridge turn left on Long Beach Boulevard and follow it to the end.

Sunrise on the northern section of Atlantic City's Boardwalk.

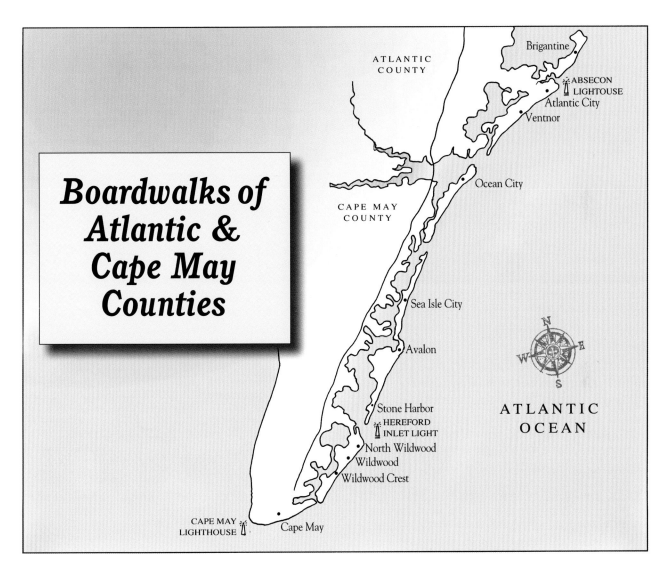

Boardwalks of Atlantic & Cape May Counties

ATLANTIC COUNTY

CAPE MAY COUNTY

Brigantine

ABSECON LIGHTOUSE
Atlantic City

Ventnor

Ocean City

Sea Isle City

Avalon

Stone Harbor
HEREFORD INLET LIGHT

North Wildwood
Wildwood
Wildwood Crest

CAPE MAY LIGHTHOUSE

Cape May

ATLANTIC OCEAN

N
W E
S

Traditional Boardwalks & Promenades

Brigantine
Length: 0.3 miles

Brigantine has the "Brigantine Bulkhead," which is essentially just that — a high, cement-topped bulkhead that stretches along the oceanfront at the north end of the town for approximately one-third of a mile. It is ten feet wide with a three-foot wide sitting area along the eastern edge, plus a few benches along the west. Beautiful Victorian lampposts line the walk and colorful dolphin containers accept trash. The bulkhead is close to the ocean and is very nicely maintained, giving one a good view of the ocean and sandy beach.

Directions:
From the north, take Garden State Parkway exit 40 to Route 30 east to Atlantic City. Follow signs to Brigantine Boulevard. Take bridge into Brigantine and follow road north to the end. From the south take exit 38 on Garden State Parkway and the Atlantic City Expressway to the end. Continue east and make a left on Atlantic Avenue, go north and make a left on South Carolina Avenue which, on crossing Route 30, becomes Brigantine Boulevard. Follow this over the bridge to the end.

Side Trips

Atlantic City Museum
At the entrance to Boardwalk Hall — the former Atlantic City Convention Center on the Boardwalk — you will find the Atlantic City Museum, filled with exhibits and large displays that highlight historical facets of the city's past.

New Jersey Korean War Memorial
While walking the Atlantic City Boardwalk make sure that you stop at the New Jersey Korean War Veterans Memorial at Park Place, the larger-than-life size statue of a soldier holding dog tags. The audio-visual programs and the memorial wall of names illustrates the contributions of these fine and heroic New Jerseyans.

Absecon Lighthouse
While on the northern part of the boardwalk, pay a visit to the restored Absecon Lighthouse. Located in the inlet section of Atlantic City at Pacific and Rhode Island Avenues, this lighthouse was built in 1857 by the same Lt. George Meade (of Civil War fame) who built Barnegat and Cape May lighthouses.

BOARDWALK AND FRONT OF BLENHEIM, ATLANTIC CITY, N. J.

The heart of the "Playground of the World," Atlantic City's boardwalk was a promenade and a midway at the same time.

Atlantic City

Length: 5 miles

This is the grandfather of all boardwalks, first built in 1870. One can begin this walk at the northern end, which is on the south sea wall along Absecon Inlet at Caspian Avenue and offers great views of the inlet, fishermen and the Absecon Lighthouse. Once you pass "Poor Man's Point" you will reach the ocean and begin walking south on the fifty- to sixty-foot wide boardwalk.

Directions:

Take the Garden State Parkway to exit 38, Atlantic City Expressway, east to the end. Follow any road east and park at any casino parking lot.

Ventnor City

Length: 2 miles

In Ventnor City the boardwalk narrows to about twenty-five feet. It looks the same as Atlantic City's but, in stark contrast to the "glitz," it passes pleasant, seaside homes. There are several shaded pavilions where one can sit and rest under the canopy. To the west you'll find beautifully landscaped residential houses, apartments and condominiums. The boardwalk passes over the surf toward the southern end and bathers can actually enjoy the sun and sea to the west of the boards. The walk ends just north of Ventnor City's southern boundary with Margate City.

Directions:

Take the Garden State Parkway to exit 38 and connect with the Atlantic City Expressway to Atlantic City. Take Atlantic Avenue south into Ventnor City. Turn left at any street. The boardwalk continues from Atlantic City.

Fun facts about *The* Boardwalk

- Atlantic City's Boardwalk is so significant it is actually considered a city street.
- It is the longest boardwalk in New Jersey — five miles in Atlantic City, and it connects to Ventnor City's two mile walk for a total length of seven miles.
- As with other early boardwalks it was orignally simple planks on the beach, placed there to keep beachgoers from bringing sand into the hotels and trains.
- Atlantic City was the first community to elevate its walkway over the beach (and waves during storms), making a permanent structure.
- The famous rolling chairs were created to ferry tourists and guests up and down the long promenade. They are still in use today.
- The Miss America Pageant celebrated the Boardwalk in its promotion, and contestants were photographed each year on the walkway until the pageant moved away from its traditional home in Atlantic City.
- Step down off the Boardwalk onto the beach and you don't have to pay a fee — Atantic City's beaches are still free!
- The board game Monopoly lets you know just how valuable — financially and culturally — the Boardwalk is. (Remember what it costs to have a hotel on Boardwalk!)

They still have rolling chairs in Atlantic City, but the pushers don't dance the way they did in 1923.

A view of the Ventnor beach and boardwalk in 1950.

Storm Torn

Ocean City wasn't far behind Atlantic City in building a boardwalk but it had a lot more trouble keeping it. The first was finished in 1887 but a winter storm the next year almost took it all away.

Then in October 1927 a fire left nothing but ashes and embers. With the summer season just months away the city started to rebuild, working six days a week (no Sundays) and ten hours a day during the worst of winter. In just four months and four days they had a new boardwalk in place and ready. It has withstood hurricanes and northeasters ever since.

View of Ocean City's boardwalk from inside a beach gift shop.

The center of Ocean City's bustling boardwalk on a summer's day.

Ocean City
Length: 2.5 miles

Just south of Great Egg Harbor Inlet lies Ocean City. Be prepared to walk the friendliest boardwalk on the Jersey Shore. You will meet many other walkers and cyclists, on-season or off. Also, in Ocean City as in Atlantic City, the restrooms are open during the off-season.

You can begin your walk just north of First Street and end at 23rd Street. The boardwalk starts out at about twenty feet wide. At 5th Street it juts out towards the sea and opens to a sixty-foot wide walkway with a great view of the Atlantic Ocean.

Amusements, movie theaters, kiddy attractions, specialty stores and restaurants line the west side of the walk. At 12th Street it narrows to twenty feet and is reminiscent of the old boardwalks, and is lined with neatly kept homes and apartments.

One unique feature of Ocean City's boardwalk are the benches along the way, many with a name plaque honoring a person or a family. Here a walker can sit, enjoy the view, and feel the warmth of the town.

Directions:

From the north on the Garden State Parkway, take exit 30; from the south, exit 29. Follow Route 52 to Atlantic Avenue. Turn left (north) to 1st Street.

Side Trips
U.S. Lifesaving Station 30 History Museum

The 19th century predecessor to the Coast Guard was the U.S. Lifesaving Service and this is one of the few remaining stations of the forty two that were built by the federal government along New Jersey's coast. Early history of brave rescues and equipment can be seen here. The Coast Guard was formed in 1915 and used the building until 1964; it was then abandoned for 13 years until citizens raised funds to preserve it. Located on the corner of 4th Street and Atlantic, this museum offers a good look into the workings of the surfmen who saved the lives of so many people caught in shipwrecks during storms along the Jersey Shore. This building was never moved, so it is hard to believe this setting was on the beach with today's homes surrounding the station.

Ocean City Historical Museum

In the Ocean City Cultural Center, 1735 Simpson Avenue, this museum offers a permanent exhibit about the history of the boardwalk, first built in 1887 and expanded over the years to include the Music Pier and other attractions. The museum is home to an extensive collection of artifacts and treasures from before Ocean City's religious founding in 1879 to the city's recent past, including an exhibit about the town's famous royal, Princess Grace.

A parasol was a must in Sea Isle City in 1910, when women tried to avoid baking in the sun.

Sea Isle City
Length: 1.5 miles

South of Corson's Inlet lies the town of Sea Isle City which has a macadam promenade that begins at 29th Street in the north and ends at 57th Street in the south. The walkway is about fifteen feet wide and sits six to eight feet above the beach. It runs atop a bulkhead close to the water's edge, and protects the many homes to the west, which appear to be below sea level. The walkway and bulkhead were built in 1963, and features heated restrooms.

Directions:

From the north, take Garden State Parkway exit 17, head east on Route 625. From the south, take exit 13, go north on Route 9 then east on Route 625. Follow Route 625 east to Central Avenue. Turn left (north) and follow to 29th Street.

Avalon
Length: 0.7 miles

Crossing over Townsend Inlet from north to south you come to Avalon, one of the quietest, prettiest towns on the Jersey shore. You can begin your walk at the north end at 21st Street and walk south to 32nd Street. Although the boardwalk is only fifteen feet wide and just over two-thirds of a mile long, it is a thoroughly pleasant walk. There is a small amusement area with no rides. The boards are centered behind a dune line which blocks a view of the ocean

Side Trips
Lucy the Elephant

The six-story building shaped like an elephant was constructed in 1881 a few miles south of Atlantic City. It is a National Historic Landmark and is located on Decatur and Atlantic avenues in Margate City.

Wetlands Institute

In Stone Harbor, the 6,000 acres of wildlife refuge and salt marsh trails offers a view of birds and their habitat. The environmental center located on Stone Harbor Boulevard also has exhibits on bird migration and salt marsh ecology.

Avalon boardwalk in the mid-1960s.

and the well-preserved natural beach area. There is also a small playground along the way with pirate ships and climbing towers. Part of the boardwalk is practically antique but most of it is of newly constructed wooden planks.

Directions:

Take Garden State Parkway exit 13. Follow Route 601 east to Avalon Avenue. Boardwalk runs from 21st to 32nd Streets.

Stone Harbor

Length: 0.2 miles

You can begin this short walk at 80th Street and First Avenue. The macadam promenade looks out over the dunes to 83rd Street. There are several benches along the way.

Directions:

From the north, take Garden State Parkway exit 10A; from the south, 10B. Follow Route 657 east to First Avenue and turn left (north) to 80th Street.

North Wildwood

Length: 0.6 miles

From the northern end of the boardwalk at 15th Street and the ocean you can head south on a wide bench-ridden boardwalk. Bordering both the east and west sides of the boardwalk are four-foot-wide cement pathways that carry the seasonal trams, which travel the length of both the North Wildwood and Wildwood boardwalks. The southern terminus of North Wildwood ends at 26th Street in the midst of a group of amusements.

Not-So-Nice Kitty

You'll find plenty to see on the boardwalks in the Wildwoods but no animal acts. But before World War II you would have seen Tuffy the lion ride in a motorcycle sidecar as it was driven around a track. But Tuffy apparently got tired of this and one day escaped from his cage, grabbed a man and dragged him under the boardwalk. Since then animal acts have been outlawed. The ban also affected alligator wrestling and a game where you threw balls at a pig to make it race.

People often dressed up to stroll the boardwalk, as seen in Wildwood in 1906.

Directions:

Take exit 6 on the Garden State Parkway to Route 147 east to 15th Street.

Wildwood

Length: 1.4 miles

The boardwalk continues in Wildwood, still twenty feet wide with the tramway on both sides. Most of the amusements are on the west side while a few structures and large piers dot the oceanside. During the season if you get foot-weary you can take a round-trip tram ride.

Directions:

Take exit 4 on the Garden State Parkway to Route 47 east. Follow to John F. Kennedy Boulevard, then left (north) to 15th Street.

Wildwood-by-the-Sea beach club looking toward Ocean Pier, 1941.

Side Trips

North Wildwood Sea Wall

A mile-plus-long sea wall has been constructed by the Army Corps of Engineers for North Wildwood. It starts at the town's northern ocean beach. The smooth top of the wall is good for walking and offers a long view of Hereford Inlet and the many sandbars.

Cape May County Park and Zoo

Directly west of Exit 11 of the Garden State Parkway lies the Cape May Zoo. This zoo houses a large variety of animals and birds. You will be surprised at the size and features of this interesting local zoo.

Ocean Drive

Ocean Drive in Cape May County is a delightful route that takes you through charming beach towns along the ocean. Enjoy the excellent views of marshes and other natural areas as you drive over the many inlet bridges between the barrier islands.

George T. Boyer Historical Museum

If you liked Wildwood and its boardwalk, a stop at this museum is a must. Located at 3907 Pacific Avenue, Holly Beach Mall in Wildwood, the museum explores the long history of this town. Special attention is given to the boardwalk, beach patrol and other organizations.

Wildwood Crest
Length: 1.0 miles

The boardwalk here is the Bike Trail, a cement walkway that runs to the east of the motels and is ideal for walking and biking. This trail is part of the beach area of the town from where small dunes and the wide, sandy beach can be viewed. The walk is at ground level, which gives the appearance that the ocean, sand and walk are all on the same plane.

Directions:

Same as Wildwood, but turn right on Ocean Avenue and left on Morning Glory Road. A cement walkway continues for another mile where the Wildwood boardwalk ends.

Cape May
Length: 1.4 miles

Cape May has a macadam promenade built on a six-foot high bulkhead at the back of the beach and provides a great view of the ocean. Walking from west to east is probably your best bet in Cape May. Before walking you may want to check the wind direction and walk with the wind at your back. At the west end you can catch a beautiful view of the Cape May Point Lighthouse and beach.

You can enjoy the view on both sides of the promenade, the ocean on one side and the town's brightly painted, gingerbread Victorian buildings on the other.

Cape May's "grand old ladies" line the streets and the beachfront walk.

There are many restaurants and lodgings along the way.

As you pass The Congress Hotel you can envision Ulysses S. Grant enjoying the Cape and the atmosphere of New Jersey's earliest shore resort.

Directions:

At the end of the Garden State Parkway follow signs into Cape May. At County Road 653 (Madison Avenue) turn left and follow to the end.

Side Trips
Cape May Historic District
Emlen Physick Estate

The city of Cape May is renowned for its well-preserved Victorian architecture. The Mid-Atlantic Center for the Arts, located at the Emlen Physick Estate, 1048 Washington Street, is an excellent place to begin when looking for information and tour schedules.

Emlen Physick Estate

Sunset Beach

A visit to Sunset Beach at Cape May Point will offer a view of a concrete ship, and you can also "dig" for Cape May diamonds on the beach. A tour of the Victorian Building in Cape May Point is also suggested.

Superstorm Sandy

On October 29, 2012, Hurricane Sandy made a meteorologically rare left turn in the ocean and brought with it an eight-foot-plus surge to the Jersey Shore, primarily north of Brigantine. This hit the boardwalks of Monmouth and Ocean counties the hardest.

The storm surge damaged the boardwalks by lifting boards and popping nails, which in turn ripped the boards from the structures and created havoc with the remaining wood framing.

In its wake, Superstorm Sandy left Seaside Park's boardwalk and amusements in ruins.

In the days following the storm, it was discovered that most of Seaside Park's composite boardwalk remained intact due to the use of screws holding the top boards. Neighboring Seaside Heights lost its entire wooden boardwalk because it was constructed with nails.

Oceanfront towns in these two counties decided to use screws to fasten the boards (wooden or composite) when rebuilding. They also added a length of metal secured to the pilings below and then to the top boards for stronger water resistance.

Time will tell if these new measures save the boardwalks in another hurricane. Beach replenishment — creating new set of sand dunes between the ocean and the boardwalks — will also help. However, these new dunes do limit views of the ocean — the very reason for the first boardwalks.

Boardwalk Memories *shared with the authors*

Seaside Heights — Famous Pizza Guy

Richy worked on the boardwalk at Henry's Playland in the late 1940s, early '50s. There was a pizza stand across from Henry's near the Casino Pier. Whenever he got a break from work, he and other workers would go to the stand and get pizza. One of the guys on the other side of the stand was friendly as he served or made the pie. Richy was told that he was an actor who was working the pizza stand between acting jobs. The gang wished him luck when he left the boardwalk that summer. Little did they know back then that Rod Steiger would be such a great movie star and boardwalk pizza guy.

Asbury Park — A Familiar Sound

John worked on an appliance wheel game on the Asbury Park boardwalk in the '60s. (Spin the wheel, win a toaster!) He remembers a "little guy" and his mother who were regular players. When they would win the guy would jump up and down and whoop and holler. This would happen all summer long and was always a spectacle. Years later, John is cooking in his kitchen and heard this familiar "whooping and hollering." He goes to his living room TV and there is that same whooping and hollering sound from Louie on "Taxi," starring Danny DeVito.

Boardwalk Surfing

Young Joe and his brother had permission from their mother to go see the surf during the hurricane of 1938. They arrived at the Seaside Park boardwalk and grabbed onto a bench just as a wave hit and broke that entire section of the boardwalk loose. Within moments the boys were on a white-water raft ride heading down the street. As the water receded the "raft" floated back and got caught on an original piling, where they hopped off their makeshift surfboard.

Seaside Park — Jump For Joy

Jack remembers the flat boardwalk in Seaside Park would be raised at the Coast Guard station. This was needed to give their amphibious vehicle a clear path to the ocean. As kids, Jack and his friends delighted in jumping off the top of the boardwalk to the sand below.

Atlantic City — Boosting Morale

During the second World War hotels along the boardwalk housed Army personnel for training and R&R. Agnes would walk the boards with her girlfriends as the "boys in uniform" would whistle at them. She said the girls would walk this route many times in order to keep up the men's morale.

Seaside Heights — MTV Preview

Maryanne worked at one of the boardwalk's ice cream stand. Whenever she got a break, she and her friends would go to the MTV's "Summer Beach House" to hear and see the latest filming for the show.

The Color Red

After author presentations we like to ask for boardwalk stories, but we joke that we want stories that are above the boardwalk not under it. When we said this a women recounted that another woman's face got so flushed that she put her hands over her face to cover the redness. We surely had struck some special memory for that lady.

Where Have All the Boardwalks Gone?

The Atlantic City Boardwalk, with the severed Heinz Pier beyond. The 1944 hurricane destroyed many boardwalks. Atlantic City chose to rebuild. Others did not.

The boardwalks lining the sandy beaches of the Jersey Shore have a timeless appeal that makes one forget their precariousness. Many have withstood the elements and daily wear and tear, but some have been lost to the ravages of the sea, and only remain as distant memories or fading photographs. Among those that remain, some began as wooden walkways that became promenades in the early twentieth century, while others became family meccas with amusement rides, games of chance, food and bath houses.

There were once boardwalks along both shores of the Raritan River, the Toms River, and many other waterways in New Jersey, but none gained the popularity of those along the Atlantic seashore in towns like Long Branch, Asbury Park, Atlantic City and

Keansburg had a boardwalk in 1916. The sender of this postcard wrote on the back: "I nearly forgot all about you."

Ocean City.

Two factors doomed oceanside boardwalks — their proximity to the sea and storms that batter the coast.

Early boardwalks were usually placed on a flattened dune line. Planners in those days weren't concerned with preserving the beach and didn't understand the role dunes play in protecting homes and keeping the beach sustainable. As a result, when strong storms or hurricanes hit the shore there was nothing to protect the boardwalks. After the elements had taken their toll, some towns rebuilt or put them on higher pilings, while others either relocated them or chose not to rebuild them at all.

The hurricane of September, 1944, and the great northeaster of March 1962 closed the chapter on some of New Jersey's boardwalks.

Bay Head in 1943.

Boardwalks of the Past

East Keansburg was the home of a promenade-type boardwalk early in the century. It had no amusements and folks strolled along the shoreline of the Raritan Bay to show off their finery. Although Ideal Beach still exists, the "boards" are history.

Hurricane Donna in 1960 did the most damage to the now-defunct Keansburg boardwalk. It also pushed water well up into the town itself. This prompted the town fathers to fill in the beachfront and build new dunes to help keep the Raritan Bay from flooding the area. Macadam was also used at this time to replace the boardwalk and the small amusement area that remains.

As in Keansburg, Laurence Harbor had a mile-long boardwalk on the bay. Here, excursion boats would dock at the pier to allow travelers to disembark and enjoy the boardwalk. A hurricane in 1955 and later storms washed the boardwalk away.

Hotel guests stroll the Beach Haven boardwalk in 1912 with acetylene gas lamps overhead. The borough's last boardwalk was destroyed in the hurricane of September 1944 and never rebuilt.

A quiet and empty Margate boardwalk in 1938.

Cliffwood Beach once had a small boardwalk; today the only remnant is a sea wall that runs a short distance, keeping the Raritan Bay from cresting into neighboring homes.

One of the earliest boardwalks on the Atlantic shoreline was in Bay Head. The town had several boardwalks over the years; now it has none.

After a storm in the spring of 1894 washed away the $258 boardwalk (which had been built to replace the one destroyed five years earlier), a wider, longer and more substantial ocean promenade was erected. It was taken up at the end of every season. Two years later, on Columbus Day weekend, a hurricane battered the beach front, tearing out bulkheads and undermining the foundations of seaside residences.

At one point the boardwalk stretched the length of the town. During World War II it sported lights reminiscent of the Victorian era. It was destroyed and

On — and under — the Stone Harbor boardwalk, circa 1900.

rebuilt time and again until most of it was destroyed by the northeaster of March 1962. The remaining boards were removed in the early 1980s never to be rebuilt.

The Beach Haven boardwalk ran almost the length of the town. Though popular with visitors, it was never rebuilt after the hurricane of 1944. Its lumber was sold to Atlantic City to repair that city's boardwalk.

Margate's boardwalk was a continuation of the Ventnor boardwalk, which was a continuation of the Atlantic City Boardwalk. It once extended all the way to Longport. It met its fate during the hurricane of 1944.

Only six or seven blocks remained, until the northeaster of 1962 took them out.

The history of Longport indicates there were several boardwalks built over the years. During World War I, a seawall was built and the boardwalk was placed inside the wall. When there was a storm, large waves would go over the wall and damage the walk. The hurricane of September 1944 and the northeaster of March 1962 assured its demise.

The boardwalk at Stone Harbor was the pride of the town, but the years took their toll. Very little of it remained after the '44 hurricane. The '62 northeaster took care of the rest.

Boardwalk Q & A

Q. *How many New Jersey boardwalks are located on the Atlantic Ocean?*
A. Twenty-eight.

Q. *Where is the longest boardwalk in New Jersey?*
A. Atlantic City, at five miles. Its boardwalk is also connected to Ventnor City's, adding an additional two miles to the walk for a total of seven miles.

Q. *What town has the shortest boardwalk?*
A. Allenhurst — 0.2 miles.

Q. *Which boardwalk is the highest?*
A. Long Branch sits on a high ridge, making it the highest walk.

Q. *Do other states have boardwalks?*
A. Today you can find some sort of boardwalk in many states — even Disney World has a boardwalk. "Classic" boardwalks are found in New York (Coney Island and the Long Island shore towns), Delaware, Maryland, Virginia, Florida, Texas, and California.

Q. *Most boardwalks rebuilt after a severe storm are placed further west, away from the encroaching ocean. Which New Jersey boardwalk was rebuilt in an easterly direction?*
A. Wildwood.

Q. *If all the New Jersey boardwalks were placed end to end, how long would they be?*
A. Almost thirty-two miles.

Q. *What boardwalk's famous pier housed entertainment, a diving bell, and a diving horse?*
A. Atlantic City's Steel Pier.

Q. *Which New Jersey town had the first boardwalk?*
A. Cape May, in 1868, was the first to lay down boards for a walk at the beach. Atlantic City followed in 1870 — but was the first to actually raise its walkway above the sand.

Q. *Why was Atlantic City's boardwalk raised and not laid flat on the sand as other boardwalks of the time?*
A. Winter storms would wash away wood lying on the sand. Atlantic City's elevated boardwalk let the storm water flow underneath the raised platform. Soon all towns adopted this design.

Q. *What is the average width of a boardwalk?*
A. Sixteen feet.

Q. *On the average, how much money do towns spend on the repairs or reconstruction of a boardwalk?*
A. $150,000 to $200,000 a year.

Fun facts about New Jersey's boardwalks

Q. *Since Superstorm Sandy how many Jersey Shore towns have rebuilt or repaired their boardwalks?*
A. All towns.

Q. *What is the name of the wood that can stand up to boardwalk wear and tear and is practically indestructible?*
A. Ipe (pronounced: *ee-pay*). It's a hardwood from the rainforests of South America. However, because of environmental concerns, many Shore towns have stopped using this wood. Currently, southern pine is the preferred material.

Q. *New Jersey's boardwalks are full of amusements. What boardwalk had the first steel Ferris Wheel?*
A. Asbury Park. It operated from 1895 to 1988.

Q. *What towns have the widest boardwalks?*
A. Asbury Park, Seaside Heights, Atlantic City, Ocean City, and Wildwood have the widest. Seaside Heights' boardwalk is seventy feet wide.

Q. *Who is responsible for the yearly care and maintenance of the town's boardwalk?*
A. Employees of the public works departments of Shore towns are the unsung heroes who work year 'round to maintain their boardwalks.

Q. *What is the old phrase that referred to someone who slept under the boardwalk?*
A. It was said that they "spent the night at the 'Underwood Hotel.'"

Q. *What boardwalk is actually a city street?*
A. Atlantic City's Boardwalk.

Somewhere beyond the amusements in Wildwood is the ocean.

*T*he following information may be helpful for those who wish to explore boardwalks on two wheels. Some towns have a different schedule during the winter months; others keep the same schedule year 'round. However, if a boardwalk is not crowded during the winter, bikes may be allowed — check with the local police department.

Bicycles on

TOWN	HOURS
Perth Amboy	Sunrise to sunset
Long Branch	Bikes prohibited
Allenhurst	Bikes prohibited
Asbury Park	6 am - 12 noon
Ocean Grove	No bikes from 10 am to 3 am
Bradley Beach	May 15 to September 15, 12 am to 10 am; September 15th to May 15th, bikes anytime
Avon~by~the~Sea	May 15 to September 15, 12 am to 9 am
Belmar	12 am to 10 am
Spring Lake	Bikes anytime from Sept. 15 to May 15. Seasonal hours 5 am to 8 am May 15 to Sept 15
Sea Girt	May 15 to September 15, 5 am - 10 am; after September 15, bikes anytime
Manasquan	6 am - 9 am all year
Point Pleasant Beach	5 am - 9 am all year
Lavallette	5 am - 10 am all year

the Boards

TOWN	HOURS
Seaside Heights	6 am - 11 am all year
Seaside Park	Summer, till 11am. Winter, anytime till 9 am where stands are located
Ocean City	Summer, 5 am to 12 noon. Winter, all day
Sea Isle City	Monday - Friday till 3 pm Sat. & Sun., before 12 noon
Avalon	Before 10 am in the summer Anytime rest of year
North Wildwood	Summer, before 11 am; winter anytime
Wildwood	6 am - 11 am all year
Wildwood Crest	Bikes anytime
Cape May	May 1 to October 31, 4 am -10 am Anytime rest of the year
Ocean Gate	6 am - 9 am all year
John C. Bartlett Jr. County Park	When open
Island Beach State Park	All year; bike trail on 8.5 mi. road

Atlantic City

No bicycles 12 noon to 4 pm, except from May 15 through September 15. Bikes permitted from 6 am to 12 noon daily. Twenty-four hour riding permitted from Connecticut Ave to Gardners Basin. On the stretch from Jackson Ave to Albany Ave riding shall be permitted from 6 am - 12 noon on Saturday and Sunday from July 1 through Labor Day, then allowed for 24 hour unrestricted use outside of those dates.

Night riders on the Ocean City boardwalk.

Acknowledgments

We gratefully acknowledge Frank Monaco, who planted the seed that grew into this book, but who wasn't able to walk with us. And no work would be very accurate if we didn't have a devil's advocate watching over us — John Van Derslice was our own personal devil. We would also like to thank all those who were kind and informative as we walked the boards. Last but not least, we would like to thank the people listed below for their generous contributions:

The Anderson Family — Jesse, Gail, Andrew; Seaside Park
Richard Billand, Laurence Harbor
Barbara Booz, "Maid of Perth", Perth Amboy
Carol Brawer, Ocean Township
Robert Bright; Wildwood Historical Society, Wildwood
John A. Camera, Borough Administrator, Seaside Heights,
Mike Cohen, Longport City Hall
Bettie Givens, Atlantic City Historical Museum, Atlantic City
Vicki Gold Levi, Atlantic City
Donna Green, Lakewood
Jay Delaney, Administrator, Seaside Park
Joseph J. Dolci, Public Works Director, Seaside Park
Karen Kronenberger, Keansburg
John Bailey Lloyd, Beach Haven
Dorothy McGough, Woodbury, N.Y.
Joe Penrose, Middletown
Frank Pescatore, Commissioner of Public Works, Long Beach Township
Allen "Boo" Pergament, Margate City Historical Society

Mike Sangiorgio, Little Silver
Tess Schwimmbeck, Seaside Park
Greg Sheeren, Public Works Director, Stone Harbor
Frank Tiemann, Margate City Historical Society
Chip Tillson, Public Works, Bay Head

Photo Credits

Photographs, unless noted below, were taken by Sal A. Marino and Dick Handschuch. All historic postcards, unless noted, are from the collection of Sal A. and Barbara Petracco Marino.
Page 5: courtesy and © Allen "Boo" Pergament
Page 22: photograph © Kelly S. Andrews
Page 36: courtesy Jenkinson's Boardwalk
Page 44: photograph © Donald T. Kelly
Pages: 7, 10, 18, 43, 46, 51, 52, 72, 73, 74, 80: photographs © Ray Fisk / Down The Shore Publishing archives
Page 62: US Fish and Wildlife Service
Page 67: courtesy and © John Bailey Lloyd collection

Promenade, Steel Pier, Atlantic City, circa 1915.

Selected Jersey Shore Bibliography

Anderson, Andrew J. *Images of America: Seaside Park*, Arcadia Publishing. 1998

Buchholz, Margaret Thomas. *Island Album—Photographs & Memories of Long Beach Island*, Down the Shore Publishing, West Creek, NJ. 2006

_____. *New Jersey Shipwrecks: 350 Years in the Graveyard of the Atlantic*, Down the Shore Publishing, West Creek, NJ. 2004

_____, editor. *Shore Chronicles: Diaries and Travelers' Tales from the Jersey Shore 1764-1955*, Down the Shore Publishing, West Creek, NJ. 1999

Buchholz, Margaret Thomas, Gingras, Sandy, et al. *Four Seasons at the Shore*, Down the Shore Publishing, West Creek, NJ. 2004

Butler, Frank. *Book of the Boardwalk*. Haines and Co., Atlantic City, New Jersey, First Edition 1952

Butler, Sylvester. SBButler Letters, August 1916. Home Page Atlantic City, Virtualac.com/boardwalk.

Cain, Tim. *Pecks Beach: A Pictorial History of Ocean City, NJ*, Down the Shore Publishing, Harvey Cedars, NJ. 1988

Coyle, Gretchen and Whitcraft, Deborah. *Inferno at Sea - Stories of Death and Survival Aboard the Morro Castle*, Down the Shore Publishing, West Creek, NJ. 2012

D'Amato, Grace Anselmo. *Chance of a Lifetime: Nucky Johnson, Skinny D'Amato and how Atlantic City became the Naughty Queen of Resorts*, Down the Shore Publishing, West Creek, NJ. 2001

Downey, Leland Wooley, Broken Spars; New Jersey Coast Shipwrecks, 1640-1935, Brick Township Historical Society, 1983

Eid, Joseph F. Trolleys *Across the Sand Dunes* Eid, J.G. 1977

Gately, Bill. *Sentinels of the Shore: A Guide to the Lighthouses and Lightships of New Jersey*, Down the Shore Publishing, West Creek, NJ. 1998

Greetings from Ocean City: Historic Postcards from America's Greatest Family Resort, Down the Shore Publishing, West Creek, NJ. 1995

Fisk, Ray and Ganss, Leslee. *All Things LBI*, Down the Shore Publishing, West Creek, NJ. 2016

Kobbe', Gustav. Jersey Coast and Pines. Short Hills, New Jersey. 1889 Gateway Press, Baltimore, MD. 1970

Liebowitz, Steve. *Steel Pier, Atlantic City: Showplace of the Nation*, Down the Shore Publishing, West Creek, NJ. 2009

Lloyd, John Bailey. *Eighteen Miles of History on Long Beach Island*, Down the Shore Publishing, West Creek, NJ. 1994

_____. *Six Miles at Sea: A Pictorial History of Long Beach Island*, Down the Shore Publishing, West Creek, NJ. 1990

_____. *Two Centuries of History on Long Beach Island*, Down the Shore Publishing, West Creek, NJ. 2005

National City Publicity Company, Atlantic City. New York, New York. 1922 [Neal, William J., et al. *Living with the New Jersey Shore*. Duke University Press. Durham, NC. 1986.]

New Jersey Cultural and Historic Guide, Department of Commerce and Economic Development, NJ Division of Travel and Tourism. 1995

Oxenford, David D. *The People of Ocean County*. The Valente Publishing House, Inc. Point Pleasant Beach, NJ. 1992

Savadove, Larry, and Buchholz, Margaret Thomas. *Great Storms of the Jersey Shore*, Down the Shore Publishing, West Creek, NJ. 2019

Turner, James Lincoln. *Seven Superstorms of the Northeast*, Down the Shore Publishing, West Creek, NJ. 1994

Wilson, Harold F. *The Story of the Jersey Shore*. The New Jersey Historical Series. D. Van Nostrand Co. Inc. New York, NY. 1964

Youmans, Rich, editor. *Shore Stories: An Anthology of the Jersey Shore*, Down the Shore Publishing, West Creek, NJ. 2004

Authors — and board walkers — **Sal Marino** and **Richard Handscuch** on the Seaside Park boardwalk.

Dubbed the "Chairmen of the Boards" by *The Trenton Times*, the authors "have turned their love of the seashore and quest for fitness into a second career of sorts as boardwalk chroniclers," observed *The New York Times*.

Trams on the Atlantic City Boardwalk.

Ocean City's boardwalk under a rainbow after a summer shower.

Down The Shore Publishing specializes in books, calendars, cards and videos about New Jersey and the Shore. For a free catalog of all our titles just send us a request:

Down The Shore Publishing
PO Box 100, West Creek, NJ 08092

email: downshore@gmail.com

www.down-the-shore.com